LIGHT AND HEAVY

by Gini Holland

Reading consultant: Susan Nations, M.Ed., author/literacy coach/
consultant in literacy development

WEEKLY READER®
PUBLISHING

Please visit our web site at: www.garethstevens.com
For a free color catalog describing our list of high-quality books,
call 1-800-542-2595 (USA) or 1-800-387-3178 (Canada).

Library of Congress Cataloging-in-Publication Data

Holland, Gini.
    Light and heavy / Gini Holland.
        p. cm. — (I know opposites)
    ISBN: 978-0-8368-8295-7 (lib. bdg.)
    ISBN: 978-0-8368-8300-8 (softcover)
    1. Weight (Physics)—Measurement—Juvenile literature. I. Title.
QC106.H65   2008
530.8'1—dc22   2007006685

This edition first published in 2008 by
Weekly Reader® Books
An imprint of Gareth Stevens Publishing
1 Reader's Digest Road
Pleasantville, NY 10570-7000 USA

Copyright © 2008 by Gareth Stevens, Inc.

Managing editor: Valerie J. Weber
Art direction: Tammy West
Graphic design: David Kowalski
Photo researcher: Diane Laska-Swanke
Production: Jessica Yanke

Picture credits: Cover (left), title page (left) © Richard Hutchings/PhotoEdit; cover (right),
title page (right), pp. 9, 16 (lower right) © David Young-Wolff/PhotoEdit; pp. 4, 5, 15,
16 (lower left) © Diane Laska-Swanke; p. 6 © Betts Anderson Loman/PhotoEdit; p. 7
© Tom Carter/PhotoEdit; pp. 8, 10 © Michael Newman/PhotoEdit; pp. 11, 16 (upper left)
© Digital Vision; p. 12 © Pat Doyle/CORBIS; p. 13 U. S. Fish & Wildlife Service; pp. 14,
16 (upper right) © Susan Van Etten/PhotoEdit

Printed in the United States of America

1 2 3 4 5 6 7 8 9 11 10 09 08 07

Note to Educators and Parents

Reading is such an exciting adventure for young children! They are beginning to integrate their oral language skills with written language. To encourage children along the path to early literacy, books must be colorful, engaging, and interesting; they should invite the young reader to explore both the print and the pictures.

I Know Opposites is a series designed to help children read and learn about the key concept of opposites. In this series, young readers learn what makes things opposite each other by exploring familiar, fun examples of things that are *Alive and Not Alive*, *Soft and Hard*, *Light and Heavy*, and *Hot and Cold*.

Each book is specially designed to support the young reader in the reading process. The familiar topics are appealing to young children and invite them to read — and re-read — again and again. The full-color photographs and enhanced text further support the student during the reading process.

In addition to serving as wonderful picture books in schools, libraries, homes, and other places where children learn to love reading, these books are specifically intended to be read within an instructional guided reading group. This small group setting allows beginning readers to work with a fluent adult model as they make meaning from the text. After children develop fluency with the text and content, the book can be read independently. Children and adults alike will find these books supportive, engaging, and fun!

— Susan Nations, M.Ed., author, literacy coach, and consultant in literacy development

The feather is light.

The rock is heavy.

The toy truck
is light.

The fire truck
is heavy.

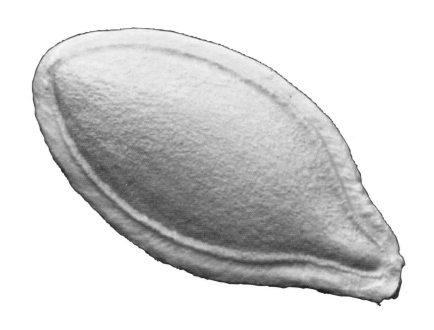

The seed is light.

The pumpkin
is heavy.

The balloon is light.

The elephant is heavy.

11

The kitten is light.

The tiger is heavy.

The leaf is light.

The log is heavy.

Which are light?

Which are heavy?